Dewdrops, Raindrops, Teardrops and Sun-drops!

Akruti Desai

BookLeaf Publishing

India | USA | UK

Presentation by *BookLeaf Publishing*

Web: www.bookleafpub.com

E-mail: info@bookleafpub.com

ISBN: 9789358314663

First edition 2024

To this last year... Last Year—the catalyst for change, the harbinger of growth, and the weaver of my evolving narrative. It transformed the very contours of my perspective. To the one who pushed me beyond the boundaries of comfort, to dance with uncertainty, to confront fears! I found seeds of new beginnings, new possibilities and a renewed sense of purpose.

ACKNOWLEDGEMENT

It is with immense appreciation and warmth that I acknowledge the invaluable contributions of those who have shaped my path.

To my father, a beacon of courage and an advocate for boldness, who instilled in me the strength to take chances and the resilience to weather the storms. Your unwavering belief in me has been a constant inspiration.

To my mother, who instilled a love for English poems and stories. She illuminates the path of caution and patience when I take a leap with an undying faith that "it will all work out fine". Your steadying influence has been a grounding force, teaching me the art of measured steps and thoughtful reflection.

To my brother, my rock solid support.

To my aunt, a motivating force and embodiment of persistence, thank you for your perpetual faith in "efforts yield enduring rewards."

To the person I was closest to: my grandmother, whose teachings on unwavering focus, the power of silence and the drive to always learn something new even in her 60s and 70s, have left an indelible mark on my life. Your lessons resonate in the spaces between the words.

To my special friends, the constellation of warmth, support, openness, and honesty, thank you for being the sounding board for my ideas, the echo chamber of my dreams, and sometimes, the gentle yet necessary confrontational force.

As I send these words into the world, I carry with me the imprints of your influence, guidance, and love. This collection is not just mine; it is a shared creation, a testament to the collective wisdom, strength, and warmth of those who have touched my life so far. A long way to go still…..

PREFACE

As thoughts and feelings are woven together, poetry emerges as an intimate expression of the human experience. As I have journeyed through the labyrinth of emotions, I have tried to pen down these thoughts during times of solitude.

Each poem is a snapshot of a moment frozen in the amber of words. I invite you to wander through these pages, to feel the rhythms of the heart, and to explore the landscapes of the mind.

The themes explored in these poems are diverse, much like the facets of life itself. From the quiet contemplation of nature's beauty to the tumultuous storms of the human heart, these verses traverse the emotional spectrum. They are an exploration of the delicate balance between light and shadow, creating a poetic chiaroscuro that mirrors the complexities of existence.

Poetry, in its essence, is a form of alchemy. It is my hope that these poems resonate with you, stirring echoes within your own experiences and inviting you to find solace, inspiration, or simply a moment of reflection. A reminder that, in the vast symphony of life, your story is a unique and valuable one.

May these verses nudge you to delve into your own emotions.

Dance of
Lights & Shadows...

On the stage of human nature's play,
A dance of lights and shadows sway.
Each heart a canvas of dark and bright,
Revealing our tangled, endless fight.
In the brilliance of compassion's glow,
Affection and love like a river flow.
We embrace the warmth, the grace, the gold,
In these moments, our spirits confident & bold.
Yet shadows lurk in the corners deep,
Where doubts and fears their secrets keep.
Envy, anger, and pride may creep,
In the silent night, when others sleep.

The canvas of life, a masterpiece,
With strokes of kindness and shades of peace.
But let us remember, we're all the same,
Both light and shadow in life's grand game.
For in understanding our dual role,
We find the light within every soul.
In this dance of lights and shadows, we see,
The beauty of human complexity.

Dewdrops & Raindrops

Dewdrops on the morning's bloom,
Glisten in the sun's soft room,
Like tiny jewels on petals' skin,
A world of wonder they usher in.
Each one a prism, a miniature sea,
Reflecting life's fragile beauty, you see.
In their brief existence, they hold a tale,
Of gentle nature, both delicate and frail.
And then there are raindrops, bold and free,
Born from clouds, they fall with glee.
A symphony of rhythm on the ground,
Nourishing the earth with a soothing sound.
Dewdrops and raindrops, of different size,
They both bring magic to our eyes.
In their quiet presence, we can find,

Nature's embellishments in every design.
Let's appreciate these gifts from above,
Dewdrops and raindrops, as tokens of love.
In their simple elegance, they remind,
That beauty in nature, we'll always find.

On learning a new language...

In the hush of a foreign tongue's catchphrase,
A journey of wonder, a linguistic chase.
Letters and sounds, so strange and new,
Learning a language, like morning's dew.
At first, it's a puzzle, a cryptic code,
But with each step, the barriers erode.
Phrases and verbs, like treasures found,
Unlocking the world, a rich, fertile ground.
With books and teachers, and practice in stride,
We dive into grammar, conjugate, and confide.
Every word learned, a bridge to explore,
New cultures, new stories, forevermore.
It's more than words; it's a gateway wide,
To new friendships and worlds, side by side.

And as we stumble, make mistakes and grow,
The language we learn becomes part of our flow.
A path to understanding, a bridge to extend,
Barriers to interactions it helps transcend
So embrace the challenge, the journeys' sweet,
In learning a language, two worlds shall meet.

Re(tro)flection

Reel back to juvenile days, after countless years,
Awkwardness and joy, mingling in tears.
Old friends & classmates, once so familiar and
near,
Now distant in memory, yet somehow dear.
In the room, a sea of changed faces,
Lives have moved on to new, distant places.
But in our eyes, a spark of recognition,
Kindles the flames of shared affection.
At first, the stiffness, like a distant storm,
Soon the laughter and stories begin to warm.
We stumble over words, but the heart knows,
The comfort of friendship, like a long-lost prose.
Moments of silence, as we navigate our
connection,

Through the layers of time, with introspection.
But then the anecdotes and shared history,
Bring back the joy, slowly unravel the mystery.
The comfort of knowing, we're not alone,
In the unwieldy dance of reconnection's tone.
For in the heart's language, we find our way,
To bridge the years, and together, we'll stay.
The pre-teen experiences, that time can't sever,
Childhood friends, in our hearts, live on forever!

Two weeks in Rameshwaram

In Rameshwaram's land of lore,
Where tales of wonder, myths galore,
Lies a secret, age-old and bold,
Of floating stones, the story's told.
A place where two seas entwine,
Bay of Bengal, Arabian Sea divine,
They meet in a dance of boundless grace,
Creating a beautiful, mystical space.
On these shores where legends reside,
The stones afloat, on waters they ride,
A testament to nature's mystic art,
Where science and wonder share a part.
Dhanushkodi, the tip of India's southern shore,

Where tales of old, they still explore.
Once a bustling town, now a memory's trace,
Lies in ruins, a tranquil, serene place.
My ma and ammama came to stay with me
For a whole week they gave me company
The next week I knew what loneliness could mean
The glorified solitude was no longer seen
No network no friends and electricity load-shedding
How little we needed to serve, live, dance and sing!
This simple life in Rameshwaram took me back in time
What it meant to pass days alone with just a few dimes

Last Days

An independent, quiet, shy & self-reliant girl
To her an unpleasant surprise life did hurl
A shadow fell, a storm came her way,
As breast cancer stole our friend one day.

She fought with courage, fierce and strong,
Through endless days, and nights so long.
But the battle was tough, the pain severe,
Our hearts filled with sorrow, our eyes with tears.

The life she lived was restrained and controlled,
In her last few days, she wanted to enjoy and be
bold
With a sinking feeling and waiting for the day

Knowing nothing you could do to keep death at
bay

In her memory, we hold moments dear,
The laughter we shared, the joy, the fear.
Though she's no more, her spirit lives on,
In our hearts and memories, she's never gone.

As we cherish the time that we've spent,
In our hearts, she's an eternal sentiment.
Believe she's in a new world, seeing a better dawn
Here, we will carry her love and friendship along

Emotions in a bottle

In the depths of my soul, emotions confined,
Like messages in bottles, kept hidden in kind.
I seal them away, these feelings so vast,
Invisible treasures of the emotional past.

The bottle, my vessel, my shield and my guard,
Holds secrets and stories, too heavy to discard.
With each cork in place, I maintain the disguise,
Yet, the heart within aches, and silently cries.

But over time, like pressure beneath the sea,
The bottled emotions, they pine to be free.
They swirl and they churn, seeking release,
A tempest of feelings that long for their peace.

For bottling up emotions, a fragile facade,
Can shatter like glass, and make the heart
flawed.
In openness and vulnerability, true emotions
reveal,
So, let us learn to uncork, to share, and to heal.

Expectations!

Under the cloud of towering expectations, I stand,
A child burdened by dreams, not always planned.
The weight of exams, like a heavy chain,
Innocence lost, replaced by pressure's reign.

To meet the world's standards, I must strive,
In the quest for success, I must survive.
Mountains of hopes, scraping the sky,
As I strive to reach, oh so high..

Amidst the demands and the unending chase,
I search for a glimpse of my true grace.
For in the midst of expectations' grasp,
I wish to find my own heart's clasp.

Let me breathe, let me dream, let me soar,
Beyond the confines of expectations' door.
A child I am, seeking my own fate,
With dreams and desires, not bound by weight.

In time, I'll learn to balance the load,
To find my own way, along this road.
For though burdened for years by massive
expectations,
Now I'll carve my own life, with my own
aspirations

Unconditional Love

In the garden of the heart, a flower blooms,
A love that transcends all the worldly dooms.
Unconditional and pure, like the morning dew,
A timeless essence, forever true.

No distance, no walls can restrain,
It's boundless power, felt in the veins.
Let it guide you, let it be your muse,
Be it a dog's cuddle or a friend's schmooze.

In the tapestry of life, threads may fray,
True is the love that's consistent, come what
may.

Through storms and sunshine, it weathers the
strife,
An unwavering beacon, the essence of life.

It's a melody that plays in the silence of night,
A symphony of stars, a celestial light.
No judgments, no conditions, just open arms,
Embracing imperfections, soothing life's harms.

A parent's gaze, a lover's touch,
Unconditional love, it means so much.
Beyond the flaws, beyond the fear,
A love that holds, always near.

In every smile, in every tear,
In joyous laughter, in silent cheer.
It's a river that flows, constant and strong,
A harmonious rhythm, a never-ending song.

Through valleys low and mountains high,
Unconditional love reaches the sky.
It's the warmth of sunlight on a winter's day,
A comforting presence that will not stray.

Victims of war...

In the silhouette of conflict and strife,
Lives forever altered, the cost of life.

War's victims, innocent and brave,
Caught in a tumultuous and relentless wave.

Their stories etched in pain and despair,
Hope they lose, it's just not fair.

Families torn, homes destroyed,
In the wake of war, hearts left paranoid.

The wounded souls, the displaced and scarred,
In the battlefield's wake, their lives are marred.

They bear the burden of a world at war,
Their resilience shining, like a forlorn star.

In unity, we must heal and restore,
The lives of war victims, who deserve much
more.

An Anxious Time

In the quiet corners of my restless mind,
Some anxiety had woven a web, undefined.

A silent storm that raged within,
A battle where no one truly can win.

It whispered worries in the dead of night,
Fuelled my fears, took flight in plain sight.

Like a penumbra, that won't let go,
Anxiety's grip, was an unwelcome woe.

The heart did race, the breath did grow shallow,
Felt an anxious grip and jittery feet below.

With time, patience and support of those close,
Learnt to overcome anxiety's chaos and repose.

Moon walk

Beneath the silver, starry cloak, we stroll,
In the quiet of the night, we are on a roll.

A moon walk, a dance in lunar grace,
A celestial adventure in immeasurable space.

With each step, we leave our earthly ties,
Gazing at the moon with wide-open eyes.

Its craters and plains, a moony art,
In this silence together, a world apart.

Moon dust beneath our careful feet,
In this cosmic waltz, our hearts beat.

Hand in hand, we explore the unknown,
In the moon's glow, our love has grown.

A sublime journey, in the magic of the night,
In our moonwalk, I find the purest light.

How Vain!

Vanity, a mirror that distorts the truth,
Reflecting only an image of youth.

In its captivating, deceptive snare,
We chase illusions, unaware.

A fleeting beauty, a shallow guise,
Vanity's mask can be our demise.

For in the endless pursuit of perfection,
We often lose our genuine reflection.

The world admires the outward sheen,
But within, the soul remains unseen.

Vanity's grip, a hollow endeavor,
Leaves the spirit wanting, forever.

Vanity's allure, though hard to resist,
Can't replace the beauty of a heart well-kissed.

We will learn as time marches on,
Vanity's facade will eventually be gone.

In the end, it's kindness and humility,
That defines true beauty and nobility.

Release the chains..

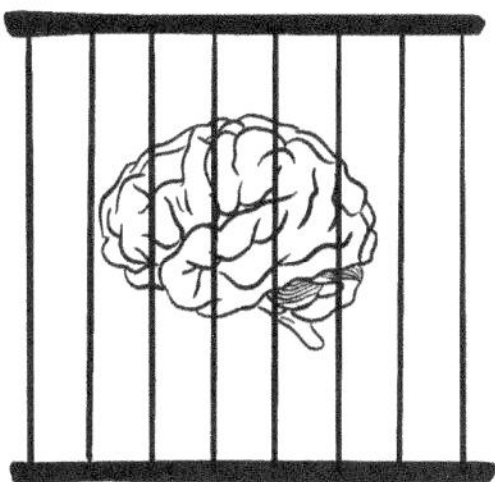

Beneath portrayal & pretence, lies a story of deceit,
Betrayal's wound, a pain so bittersweet.

Promises broken, trust broken asunder,
In the dark, a heart left to wonder.

A dagger forged in murmurs soft,
Pierces the armor of love aloft.

A web of lies, like a sieve so fine,
Woven by someone called "mine."

In the fortress of dreams, a breach appears,
As trust crumbles, drowned in silent tears.

In whispers hushed & secrets kept,
Faith was lost, as the heart wept.

Yet, from this darkness, we must rise,
To mend our souls, to look at the skies.

Perfidious partners, a painful strife,
But in time, we'll find our way back to life.

Release the chains, let forgiveness flow,
For in letting go, true strength will grow.

Despite the echoes of a betrayed past,
An intrepid spirit is free at last.

Stronger we stand, with lessons learned,
Knowing, in a different direction, our hearts are
returned.

With another human you again can sing a song
A dawn, a metamorphosis, a soul reborn!

A bitter irony..

In the cycle of life's relentless sway,
The oppressed, at times, become oppressors,
they say.

A bitter irony in the human tale,
As roles reverse, and humaneness may fail.

Once victims of cruelty, now wielding the rod,
The oppressed turned oppressors, a twist so odd.

Seeking power, revenge, or control,
They lose their empathy, their gentle soul.

Breaking the cycle, a challenging quest,
Not losing your moral compass, to do your best.

Let not the pain and suffering go in vain,
Build something new, not seek revenge.

Stolen Childhoods

In a different home where they reside,
Orphans with dreams, they try to hide.
Stolen childhoods, security torn,
In a life so tough, they are reborn.
No mother's love, no father's care,
In this world, it's not always fair.
Through tears and struggles, they find their way,
Trying to build bonds that won't decay.
For in each other, they've found their kin,
Together, they'll fight and strive to win.
Stolen childhoods, but hope remains,
In their hearts, it burns like flames.
Let's reach out a hand, lend a caring touch,
For these stolen childhoods, we care so much.
To heal their wounds, help dreams to thrive,
Orphans, with love, they'll surely survive!

Hard conversations

In the plights of heavy hearts we find,
Conversations burdened, like an anchor's bind.
The power of words, both truth and fear,
Rests upon our shoulders, all so clear.
When we must address the truths untold,
Confront the demons that we hold.
The gravity of these discussions, deep,
Is a weight that we must bear, our secrets to
keep.
The silence, a shroud that hides the pain,
But honesty and courage break the chain.
For when we dare to share what's true,
The burdens lessen, and the skies turn blue.
In vulnerability, we find our strength,
And bridges built across the chasm's length.
We must not shy away from what's hard,

By not having the talk, growth is charred.
Lifting the weight off & having "the talk",
though heavy,
Helps our understanding, and a world less
unsteady.
Anger, awkwardness, sorrow, anxiety all in a
caisse,
Only in a melting pot of dialogue can we
displace!

A New Year!

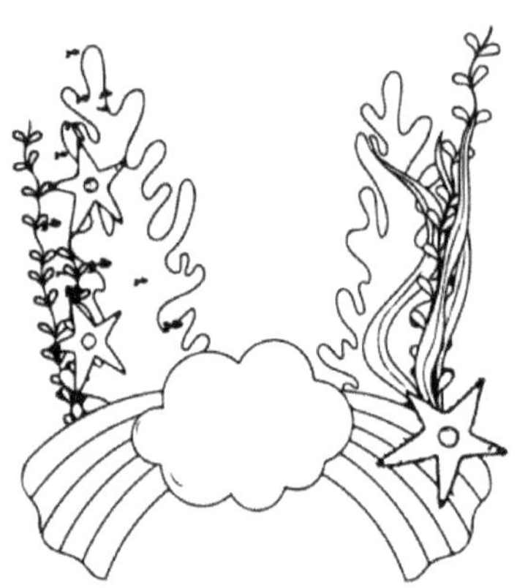

At every New Year, at every new Gregorian
calendar birth,
Resolutions are plenty, of those there is no
dearth,
Shed its skin, a snake must, many times a year,
By rubbing against something abrasive, till it
causes a tear,
Not a painful process, yet they hide;
uncomfortable,
Undisturbed we must leave them when they are
vulnerable
A crab instead fills itself with water, so it swells,
Expand it does till a crack shows in its shell,
To unbury out of sand, days they take more,

Leave us alone for that while, they implore!
Imagine Humans! Who never shed their skin as
a whole,
A process more complex and vulnerabilities
galore,
Give them time and show the inclination to
unearth,
On this fast-paced world, value their worth,
Have patience as they accept a disturbed past
they can't change,
Develop an unyielding conviction, years of
drought can be tailed by rain!
Washing the dust away of yesteryears, with the
gentleness of morning dew,
And take a look at humanity with eyes anew!
One man's hope need not be another's despair,
If we all come together and begin to share.
With a conscience and wisdom, if we use the
past,
To open a doorway to a blissful world that will
last
As turning over a new leaf, simple it may be not,
Yet like a Kalpavriksha, isn't it a salubrious
thought?!

I'll always be there…

No masks, no pretense, just honest and sincere,
A connection that deepens, drawing near.

In a realm of illusions and fleeting desire,
We seek a flame that will never tire.

Not just a spark, but a steady flame,
A love untainted, bearing no shame.

A love that withstands the test of time,
A hymn composed in a rhythm sublime.

Through seasons of joy & stormy weather,
We stand united, hand in hand, forever.

Through wrinkles of time and silver in hair,
Growing old together, a love beyond compare.

As years unfold, and memories accrue,
Our bond deepens, steadfast & true.

A philharmonic composed of trust and care,
True love whispers," I'll always be there"

So let it be your guiding compass,
A timeless journey, one that will last.

Is it a nebula?

Is it a whisper in Zephyr's embrace?
Or the gentle rain on a soft moonlit face?

Mysterious, elusive, like ethereal mist,
Is it a dream that can't be kissed?

Yet within its haze, a brilliance glows,
A radiant energy that forever flows.

In the cosmic journey where stars align,
Love's nebula emerges, divine.

A force magnetic, an undying art,
Is love nebulous, or a flame from the heart?

Letting go…

In the corridor of time, echoes linger,
Whispers of the past, like ghostly fingers.

Yet, a decision stirs, a courageous art,
To step away, leaving the past to depart.

Footprints of yesterday on sands,
Washing away as tide commands.

Let the shadows of the past disperse,
As the sun of the present begins to immerse.

The weight of regrets, like stories untold,
Release them gently, let them unfold.

Bid farewell to what was once known,
To the seeds of nostalgia that were sown.

A horizon ahead, a promise unseen,
A future unveiled, beautiful & pristine.

What matters to you?

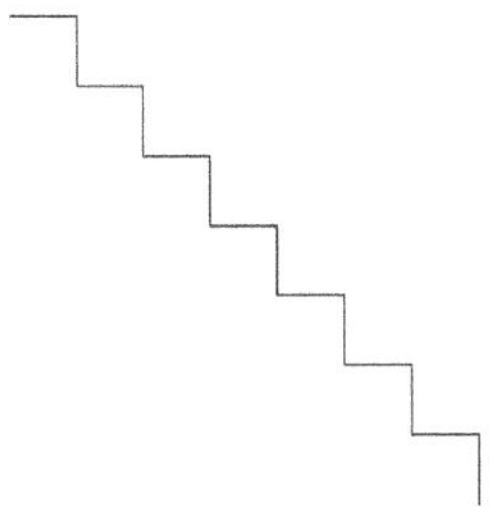

Success, a ladder to reach the heights,
Happiness, the warmth of shared delights.
In the pursuit of success, we may strive,
But happiness resides in the way we jive.
Success often measured with wealth and fame,
Happiness finds joy in life's simple game.
In trophies won or fortunes amassed,
Happiness blooms in moments that last.
Success can be fleeting, a fickle prize,
A happy memory in hearts, it never dies.
It's in love, in laughter, moments of grace,
In life's simple pleasures, it finds its place.

So, remember, dear soul, as you chase your
dream,
Success and happiness are not what they seem.
For success, in its glory, can leave you cold,
While happiness, in your heart, is pure gold.

Filter kaapi

In Southern lands, where palm trees sway,
A cup of filter coffee starts the day.
Ground beans, in a metal sieve,
Hot water poured to make it live.
Filtered through with patience and care,
In every cup, a love affair.
In homes and cafes, it's a common sight,
Served with milk, or just black as night.
From Madras to Mysore, it's known so well,
In every corner, its stories tell.
Filter coffee, a cultural treasure,
A morning ritual that brings such pleasure.
In Matunga's heart, a vibrant place to be,
Where filter coffee flows, rich and free
From the bustling markets to leafy lanes,
Filter coffee here forever reigns.
With a blend of flavours, bold and smooth,
It's the essence of mornings that we all approve.
So raise your cup, let's toast and cheer,
To filter coffee, oh so dear ☺

Not a day..

Your memory, a star in my endless sky,

In every thought, you're the reason why.

Through the seasons, as time does flow,

Your presence in my heart continues to grow

In laughter and tears, you're always near,

An everlasting memory, so crystal clear.

With each dawn's light and twilight's kiss,

It's your love I long for, your sweet bliss.

So, in the silence, I'll hold you tight,

For in my thoughts, you're my guiding light.

Not a day shall pass, my dear, without,

Your memory, love, and fervent devout.

www.ingramcontent.com/pod-product-compliance
Lightning Source LLC
LaVergne TN
LVHW021256200726

843509LV00012B/1696